HEAD INJURIES

HEAD INJURIES

Nathan Aaseng
and Jay Aaseng

A Venture Book
FRANKLIN WATTS
A Division of Grolier Publishing
New York London Hong Kong Sydney
Danbury, Connecticut

MAB EG
Photographs copyright ©: A/P Wide World Photos: pp. 11, 27, 40, 47, 86; Photo Researchers: pp. 17 (Scott Camazine), 21 (Larry Mulvehill), 30 (MVI/SS), 31 (Department of Clinical Radiology, Salsburg District Hospital/SPL), 50 (Michael Hayman), 59 (Alexander Tsiaras/SS), 66 (Medivisuals/SS), 82 (Spencer Grant), 95 (Roberta Hershenson); The Bettmann Archive: pp. 24, 25, 43, 57, 92; Reuters/Bettmann: p. 45; SuperStock: p. 60; Long Island Jewish Medical Center: p. 61; Photofest: p. 98 (Francois Duhamel).

Library of Congress Cataloging-in-Publication Data

Aaseng, Nathan.
Head injuries / by Nathan Aaseng and Jay Aaseng.
p.   cm. — (A Venture book)
Includes bibliographical references and index.
Summary: Provides information about traumatic brain injuries, including causes, diagnosis, treatment, rehabilitation, how to decrease risk, and how to help people affected.
ISBN 0-531-11267-5
1. Brain—Wounds and injuries—Juvenile lierature. [1. Brain—Wounds and injuries.]
I. Title.
RD594.A226 1996

617.4'81044—dc20   95-44988 CIP AC

CONTENTS

1
Instant Nightmare
9

2
The Silent Epidemic
20

3
What Goes Wrong
29

4
Who's at Risk
38

5
What You Should Do
49

6
Emergency Diagnosis and Treatment
54

7
Long-term Problems
65

8
Rehabilitation
78

9
Attacking the Problem
90

Glossary
101

Bibliography
105

Source Notes
107

Index
109

HEAD INJURIES

1

INSTANT NIGHTMARE

Your brain is an intricate bundle of cells that holds the key to who you are, to everything that makes you a unique human being. Most of us take this marvelous piece of evolutionary engineering for granted, and take few special precautions to protect it. The nightmare of traumatic brain injury always catches us unprepared. One moment everything seems perfectly fine. It is a bright, sunny day and you are enjoying it. An instant later you are involved in an unforeseen accident that has injured your head. Now, you are fighting for your life.

My son, Jay, was 13 when he experienced the instant transition from a peaceful, carefree existence to the life-threatening and self-threatening world of traumatic brain injury:

> *I was camping at a youth group retreat in Chetek, a small town in northern Wis-*

consin. Actually, I hadn't really wanted to go, but my parents insisted on it. Once I was there, I had lots of fun hiking across the frozen lake, cross-country skiing, having snowball fights, and stuff like that.

One day we found a humongous inner-tube and immediately headed for the steepest hill we could think of. So what if there happened to be a huge tree at the bottom? At first, we took turns cruising down the hill. Since nobody could get going fast enough to make it to the tree, it posed no threat.

Then someone had a great idea. He suggested that all six of us pile into the innertube and go down the hill at once. We jumped on, pushed off, and flew down the hill at the speed of light—or so it seemed. We realized, too late, that we were heading for the tree and easily had enough momentum to hit it at top speed. We braced for the collision. When we hit the tree, our innertube bounced back about 10 feet (3.5 m) and then flipped over.

Luckily, no one was hurt. Undaunted by our near miss, we climbed the hill and tried again. No one wanted to stop. We were flirting with danger, and having the time of our lives.

The next day, a few of us finished packing and cleaning the cabin about an hour before we were supposed to go home. We went outside not really knowing what we would do.

We found the innertube at the bottom of

High-speed thrills run the risk of collisions that can instantly change fun into a nightmare.

the big hill. We all wanted to go down the hill a couple more times, but we didn't feel like risking such a dangerous hill. We decided to walk back toward the cabin to look for a better one.

We didn't have much luck finding a hill with no trees. We finally came across a hill with a perfect incline. Unfortunately, it was covered with trees. All of us knew that no one in their right mind would go down that hill, but we were tired of searching and decided to go down it anyway. We jumped into the innertube and pushed off. There were many trees, and to my horror, we were picking up speed very quickly. I closed my eyes and hoped for the best. Amazingly, we missed every one.

Just as I was about to breathe a sigh of relief, I realized that we were heading straight for a ledge. Below it was the frozen lake. Somebody bailed out, but the rest of us sailed off the ledge and onto the ice.

Because traumatic head injuries scramble the memory-creating ability of the brain, few of the people who experience such injuries can recall the actual event. Jay lost consciousness when his head struck the ice and so, for a time, his recollection of the incident became distorted.

Miraculously, no one was hurt. We all scrambled back up the hill and went searching for a new location. Then everything got very

*weird. Somebody yelled, "Timberrrrr!" and a
huge tree came crashing down in front of us.
We looked around and took off into the woods.
Then, for some unknown reason, I could
hardly run at all. Even though I yelled at the
others to wait, they kept running. I found
myself hopelessly lost in the woods. Birds started chirping insanely, and something was
rustling in the bushes.*

*All at once there was a brilliant display
of lights in the sky, and though I couldn't
make out the words, someone seemed to be
speaking to me. ". . . Come on, Jay. . . . You'll
be okay. . . . That was quite a fall. . . ."*

*As I pulled out of this confusing dream,
I slowly opened my eyes and realized that a
man, probably one of the chaperones, was
helping me walk up the hill.*

At this point, Jay had recovered enough from
the initial jolt to regain awareness of his surround-
ings.

*Finally the gears in my head started to
turn and I realized that we must have
crashed, and that I must have been unconscious. I felt a searing jolt of pain in my right
leg, which caused me to collapse. I realized I
must have been seriously hurt.*

*Somebody carried me to the cabin, and
laid me on the couch. I had an awful head-
ache, and was just beginning to fall asleep*

when someone told me that it was time to leave. On the 45-minute drive back to Eau Claire, I suddenly felt extremely nauseous. As soon as the driver pulled over, I stepped out and lost my breakfast.

When I picked Jay up at the parking lot, I was told that he had banged up his head in a sledding accident. No one was aware that he had lost consciousness, and I wasn't told that he had vomited. His legs wobbled and he seemed woozy as I helped him into our car. I decided to take him home and keep a close eye on him until he improved.

I began to feel a little better, but just before we got home, I felt a sonic boom go off inside my head, and an explosion as painful as a sledgehammer smashing into my skull. I threw back my head and screamed.

That scared me. Immediately, I headed for the nearest hospital. I wanted to speed down the street and take the corners fast, but I had to go slow to keep Jay from feeling worse. Even then, we had to stop twice during the one-mile trip for him to vomit. As soon as Jay was admitted, I had to make an awful call to my wife, Linda.

By the time we arrived at the hospital, the initial burst of pain was gone. I felt very weak and fatigued. I must have been drifting into unconsciousness because my sur-

roundings were nothing but a blur of mixed images.

For the next couple of hours, everything was a blur. I wish I could describe what was going on at the time, but I really didn't have the faintest idea what was happening to me. Needles were being poked into me. I felt myself being whisked around on a moving cart from room to room, as test after test was performed. The nurses were constantly saying, "It'll be all right, you'll be okay." The doctors were shouting gibberish.

The medical staff rushed Jay by ambulance across town to a hospital that had better facilities to treat brain injuries. When Linda and I arrived, we were greeted by a chaplain and a neurosurgeon in his hospital greens. The surgeon explained that a CT scan had detected bleeding under the skull. He wanted our permission to operate. That was the only way to stop the bleeding and remove the pooling blood.

"And if you don't operate?" we asked, almost too numb to speak.

"It'll kill him."

There was no time to lose.

I vaguely remember a ride in an ambulance, and my parents telling me that I was going to be operated on.

As I was wheeled into the operating room on a rather uncomfortable tablebench,

15

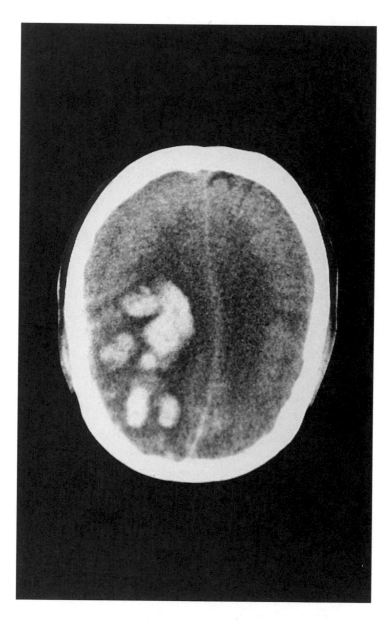

A CT scan picks up an area of bleeding beneath the skull.

many things were going through my mind. I thought about what had happened, and how stupid I had been. Most of all, I just wished I could have a second chance. As the doctor injected the anesthesia through my IV, everything started to fade away. I just hoped I'd live through it all. Then everything went black.

There is no more helpless feeling in the world than pacing in a hospital waiting room for 2 hours while a surgeon performs an emergency brain operation on your son. I thought about a friend who had suffered severe brain damage from an infection. I remembered the shock of seeing her for the first time at the hospital. The once healthy, active, intelligent camp counselor was gone, and in her place was someone I didn't recognize. She had become a person with no control over her emotions. She could not talk or feed herself. Would this happen to Jay?

I woke up in a bed, the awful smell of anesthesia in the air. I was relieved to see my operation had been successful. I learned that I had been very lucky. I had come pretty close to, well, ascending to a higher calling. If I hadn't screamed when I did, my dad would have driven me home instead of to the hospital. By the time someone discovered the bleeding, I would certainly have suffered serious brain damage and possibly death.

At first, Jay had no attention span. He had trouble conversing, and could not concentrate enough to watch his favorite television program. I brought his Nintendo system to his hospital room, but he could not focus on that either. No words can express the relief we felt when he began to recover. After 3 days of steady improvement in the hospital, he returned home and was able to play his piano recital piece from memory.

For a while, I had 48 staples in my head. After the accident, I had to quit all contact sports and many other recreational activities, including diving, for a year.

It's been 2 years since my accident. Looking back on the whole thing now is very confusing. It's hard for me to say exactly how this incident has changed my life. When I think about the past, I always refer to "the time before" and "the time after." I don't have trouble with memories, but I do have trouble remembering what I used to be like before the accident. I have become more irritable and have temper flares. I often use bad judgment and tend to act on the spur-of-the-moment. I am still trying to cope with the changes.

I'll never forget my near miss with death. What frustrates me the most is how easily the accident could have been prevented. Fun is fun, but taking deadly risks is stupid.

After you die, there aren't any second chances. The accident could have happened to anybody. People don't realize how easy it is to cross the line between something that is fun and something that can kill you.

2

THE SILENT
EPIDEMIC

Unfortunately, what Jay experienced happens all too often, frequently with even more serious consequences. Among Americans between 1 and 19 years old, accidents cause more deaths than all diseases combined. The majority of these accident-related deaths are the result of a *traumatic brain injury*. Traumatic brain injury can be caused by sudden impact with an object or violent movement of the brain against the skull.

Each year, roughly 2 million Americans, about half of whom are children, enter hospital emergency rooms for the treatment of traumatic brain injuries. Between 10 and 25 percent of the individuals treated for brain injuries are diagnosed as having moderate to severe damage.

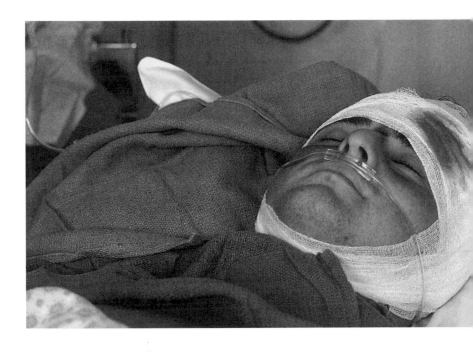

*This head injury is serious enough
to require hospitalization.*

The impact of traumatic brain injuries on society is staggering. More than 100,000 Americans die annually. At least 2,000 of those who live are reduced to a permanent vegetative state. Between 16,000 and 20,000 suffer severe temporary or permanent disabling injury. Another 70,000 to 90,000 people endure life-long loss of some brain function.

The lifetime cost of caring for a person with a severe brain injury averages more than $5 million. The annual cost for rehabilitation of Americans with brain injuries exceeds $4 billion. More money is spent to treat people with traumatic brain injuries than any other medical condition except cancer.

Even when patients have only mild symptoms of traumatic brain injury, they may experience subtle changes in their behavior and thought processes. These changes can make life miserable for the individuals and their friends and families. Experts estimate that only 5 percent of people with traumatic brain injuries get the help they need.

Even the people who experience a brain injury may be oblivious to the consequences. Many brain injuries go unreported because people believe that a bump on the head is like a bad bruise to the shin—painful but not something that needs treatment.

In a celebrity-conscious society, high-profile individuals who suffer health problems often attract attention and bring about a public awareness of the problem. That has not been the case with traumatic brain injuries. Nationally known people have experienced brain injuries ranging from mild to disabling to fatal, from a wide variety of causes. Yet their ordeals have done little to educate people about head injuries.

Many sports celebrities have suffered traumatic brain injuries in the line of duty. On January 23, 1994, two of the country's most popular sports heroes suffered similar brain injuries on the same afternoon. First, Kansas City Chiefs' quarterback Joe Montana had to be helped off the field after a hard tackle by three Buffalo Bills bounced his head against the frozen artificial turf.

A few hours later, Dallas Cowboys' quarterback Troy Aikman ducked his head into the knee of onrushing San Francisco lineman Dennis Brown. Aikman left the game with a concussion and was so confused that he could recall only one play from the entire first half. He suffered headaches and had trouble sleeping for the next few days. People joked about his loss of memory.

The list of prominent athletes who have suffered traumatic brain injuries is long. The Boston Bruins' star defenseman, Ted Green, was nearly killed when a hockey stick struck him in the head during a fight on the ice.

Millions of television viewers watched as gold-medal winner Greg Louganis hit the back of his head on a diving board while qualifying for the finals of the 1988 Olympic springboard-diving competition. A similar accident killed a top Russian diver just a few years earlier.

Boxers routinely suffer traumatic brain injuries during their fights. Former light-heavyweight boxing champion Jose Torres said the sensation of taking a hard punch is "like one million ants get into your brain and into your whole body."[1]

Traumatic brain injuries from automobile accidents have claimed many well-known victims. Jan Berry, of the popular surf rock duo Jan & Dean (*Little Old Lady from Pasadena*), plowed his Corvette into a parked car and fell into a coma in 1967. The

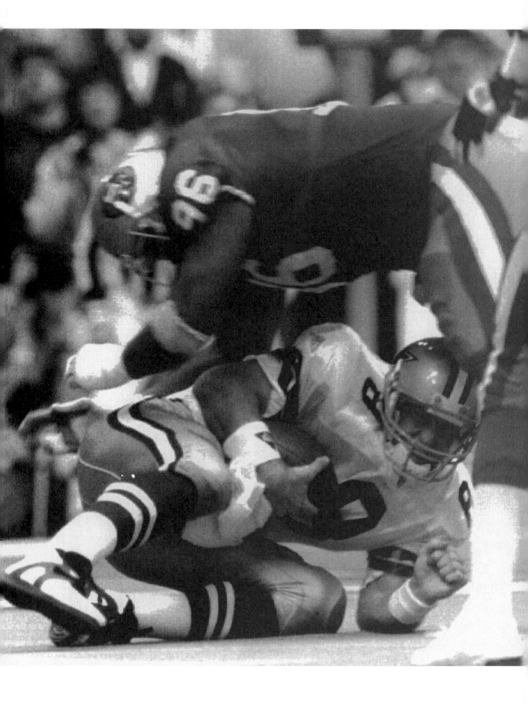

Millions of television viewers winced as champion diver Greg Louganis smacked the diving board in the 1988 Olympic Games held in Seoul, South Korea.

(Facing page) *Even a helmet cannot protect Dallas Cowboys' quarterback Troy Aikman from suffering a concussion when a San Francisco 49ers' knee strikes his head in this playoff game.*

brain damage prevented him from recording and touring at the peak of his popularity. Although he resumed singing following several years of rehabilitation, his career was never the same.

Nancy Cruzan, a 25-year-old Missouri woman, became the centerpiece of a national debate over a person's right to die after an automobile accident left her brain dead. The battle over whether or not Cruzan's parents had the right to remove life-support technology went all the way to the U.S. Supreme Court in 1990.

Traumatic brain injury caused by violent acts are also common. Influential African-American writer and former Black Panther leader Eldridge Cleaver suffered a brain hemorrhage on March 1, 1994, following a mugging attack.

In 1980, President Ronald Reagan's press secretary, James Brady, fell victim to a traumatic head injury caused by a gunshot wound. He was struck by an assassin's bullet meant for Reagan. Although Brady survived, the bullet severely damaged the right side of his brain. He lost the ability to move in his left arm and leg. He also experienced short-term memory loss and slurred speech. Brady and his wife have since become leaders in a national campaign for gun control.

Perhaps the most famous criminal case of the century involved a brain injury. On November 22, 1963, President John F. Kennedy died of massive head wounds caused by rifle shots.

Traumatic brain injuries are one of the most widespread, serious, and devastating health hazards

*James Brady speaks in favor of legislation to control
the spread of assault-style firearms.*

facing Amcricans today. Yet the health issues related to head injuries are largely ignored and widely misunderstood. No wonder head injury survivors, their families, and other advocates call head injuries the *silent epidemic.*

3

WHAT GOES
WRONG

The human brain is an enormously complex master-control center made up of billions of nerve cells, which are connected to a network of nerves located throughout the body.

The brain receives messages in the form of electrical impulses from all over the body, and processes the information they provide. The brain has the ability to store information or thoughts for future use, an activity called *learning*. These thoughts can be retrieved when needed, a process called *memory*.

The brain makes judgments based on the information it receives and on thoughts that it recalls, and then sends out signals that regulate all of the body's responses, from muscle movement to emotions to speech.

While certain functions are controlled by

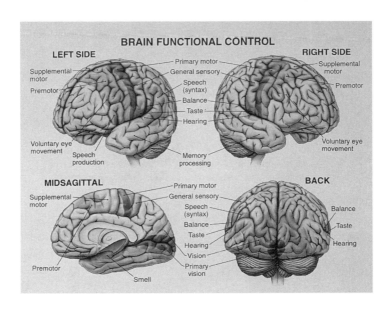

These drawings show which areas of the brain control specific functions.

specific areas of the brain, no part of the brain operates independently of the other parts. The components of the memory system and emotional system, in particular, are scattered throughout the brain. The various areas are connected by nerve fibers that run throughout the brain.

Unfortunately, this absolutely essential organ is rather delicate. If bleeding or swelling of brain tissue stops the flow of blood to the brain for just a few minutes, enough cells will die to cause brain damage or even death. Jarring can disrupt the nerve network of the brain or cause a person to lose consciousness.

THE BODY'S DEFENSES FOR THE BRAIN

Few people would survive for long if their brains were not well protected against injury. The body guards this vital organ with more armor and cushioning than is found anywhere else in the body. The primary protection is the skull, a bone that surrounds the soft tissues of the brain. The skull absorbs, disperses, or deflects most of the force of any blow. Sometimes the force of a collision can be great enough to crack the bone, causing a *skull fracture*, yet because the skull has absorbed so much of the force, the brain is left relatively unscathed.

The open spaces in the brain are filled with

This X-ray image shows a dark, horizontal line at the center left, indicating a fracture of the skull.

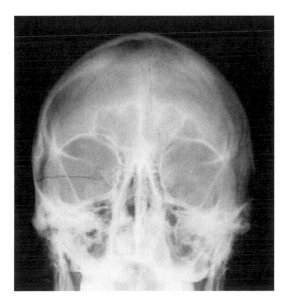

cerebrospinal fluid, which acts like an airbag to cushion blows to the head. The brain is also covered with three layers of thin material called membranes. The strongest of these, the dura, lies just inside the skull.

Nearly everyone, especially as children, suffers blows to the head without suffering any damage. Because the skull and the brain cushioning work effectively, most of these blows cause no problems.

TYPES OF HEAD INJURIES

While the built-in safety devices work well to prevent injury, they are far from invincible. There are many types of brain injuries that can overwhelm or slip past the skull and the body's other protective measures.

Brain injuries are divided into two main categories: *congenital nervous injury* and *acquired brain injury*. Congenital nervous injury refers to brain damage or malfunction that is already present at birth. Such conditions include cerebral palsy.

Acquired brain injury refers to those brain injuries that are not present at birth but develop due to some outside factor or event. Acquired brain injuries can be caused by an interruption of blood flow to the brain. Brain cells die because the circulatory system is unable to supply them with oxygen. This condition, known as *anoxia*, can be triggered by a near-drowning or sudden rupturing of a blood vessel (known as a *stroke*).

TYPES OF ACQUIRED BRAIN INJURIES

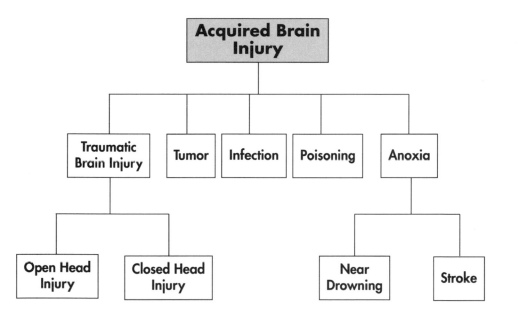

Brain tumors, infections from diseases such as *encephalitis* and meningitis, and poisoning are other sources of serious, often fatal, acquired brain injury.

This book deals primarily with the type of acquired brain injuries known as traumatic brain injuries, which are caused by a blow to the head or the result of violent shaking or jarring.

There are two kinds of traumatic brain injuries: *open head injuries* (sometimes called penetrating head injuries) and *closed head injuries*.

An open head injury occurs when a small object pierces the skull and enters the brain tissue. This usually occurs with gunshot wounds. Because damage from such an injury is usually restricted to the area penetrated by the object, the effects of the wound are somewhat predictable and depend on the function of the damaged area of the brain. Widespread damage is usually fatal. Unlike closed head injuries, open head wounds introduce the risk of infection.

Closed head injuries damage the brain, even though the skull is left intact. The most common result of a traumatic closed head injury is a *concussion*. In a concussion, the brain is jostled inside the skull. In many cases this jostling effects the brain stem, causing the victim to lose consciousness. The brain may also be injured by striking the skull's inner bony bumps, which hold the brain in place.

Immediately following a brain injury, new cells are called into action to replace damaged ones. The person who has sustained the brain injury may be disoriented until the cells adjust to the new demands.

The more severe the blow, the more the brain is jarred and the greater the damage it sustains. In a mild concussion, the person may not lose consciousness or may recover it in a few seconds or minutes. A severe concussion may leave an individual unconscious for days or even months, a condition known as a *coma*. The length of time a person remains unconscious is one indicator of the severity of the damage to the brain.

A sudden impact great enough to cause a concussion almost always produces shock and disturbs the memory-creating centers of the brain. As a result, few people who survive a traumatic brain injury remember the actual event.

Most traumatic brain injuries occur when a person in motion comes to a sudden stop, usually as a result of colliding with something. The force of a blow can slam the brain into the skull, which causes two types of problems. Firstly, this impact can damage the *cortex*, the surface of the *cerebrum* in which most of the brain's activity takes place.

Second, it can cause tears or *lacerations* in the brain tissue and can break blood vessels. Broken blood vessels that are too small to cause much bleeding may leave a bruise known as a *contusion*. When larger blood vessels break they may bleed or *hemorrhage*. The flowing blood may collect in a pool called a *hematoma*.

There are two dangers from contusions, hemorrhages, and hematomas. First, these injuries may interrupt the blood supply to brain cells, resulting in anoxia. Second, they stimulate swelling in the brain tissue. Whenever tissue is damaged, the body reacts by sending more blood to the injured areas. Normally, this extra blood is good because it increases the rate of healing, but it also produces swelling.

The skull, however, has little room to accommodate the swelling. While a smashed thumb expands in response to swelling, swollen brain tissue can only exert greater pressure on the surrounding tissue. Increased intracranial pressure (pressure within the skull) may pinch off the blood flow in the brain. Swelling reactions are the most common cause of serious brain injury.

The effects of closed head injuries are difficult to predict or diagnose because the damage is not confined to the immediate area of cell destruction. An injury known as *coup contre coup* affects not only the immediate area of impact, but also the area opposite the point of the impact. The force of the blow causes the brain to bounce into the skull. The result is bruising, bleeding, and swelling.

Traumatic brain injuries can also disrupt a person's mental processes by altering chemical and electrical balances within the brain. Both swollen tissue and scar tissue formed by dead cells can trigger these changes. *Seizures* may occur as a result of altered *electrochemical* activity in the brain.

The most common and disabling type of brain injury, the *diffuse axonal injury*, cannot be traced to a specific location. It occurs when a jarring impact tears, twists, or stretches microscopic blood vessels and nerve cells, fibers, and connections throughout the brain. The instant deceleration of an auto accident or slamming into a tree can produce this effect, even if the skull does not actually strike an object. These connections between blood vessels may never be properly reestablished.

Just where in the brain this shearing occurs in any given accident is anyone's guess. It would be like covering the city of Los Angeles with a shield (skull) and then trying to determine from the outside exactly which structures have been affected by an earthquake. Diffuse axonal injuries may produce a dramatic change in the brain's function or, more commonly, a less noticeable general loss of efficiency.

Some parts of the brain are more likely than others to sustain damage simply because they lie in a more vulnerable location. The brain stem is often injured because it can be violently twisted or pulled. The frontal lobe of the cerebrum is also a common site of injury because the victim is facing forward during most high-speed collisions. The relatively well-protected cerebellum and the occipital lobe in the back of the skull are least likely to sustain damage.

But while damage to certain areas can produce predictable injuries and impairments, such phenomena as the coup-contre-coup impact, altered electrochemical states, and diffuse axonal injury make the consequences of traumatic brain injuries as erratic as the effects of a dropped radio. In some cases, the fall will cause no damage. In other cases, the fall may loosen a connection or two, creating a minor problem. It is also possible that the radio will not work at all without major repairs.

Similarly, a person who suffers a bump on the head without even losing consciousness may occasionally end up seriously impaired, while another person may walk away from a frightening collision with no apparent damage.

4

WHO'S AT RISK?

Traumatic brain injuries occur when the head encounters a greater amount of force than its defensive structures are able to withstand. There are four primary factors that determine the extent of the force that the head encounters: velocity, weight, sharpness, and hardness.

Who will suffer a more serious head injury: a person who walks into a tree, one who runs into a tree, or one who slams into a tree while speeding on a motorcycle? The greater the velocity—the speed at which an object travels, the worse the injury. Because velocity influences force more than any other factor, race-car drivers have a very high rate of brain injury.

It is difficult to imagine a family more familiar with the horror of motor-vehicle brain injury than the Allison racing clan. In August 1993, Clifford Allison died of head injuries sustained during a high-speed crash at the Michigan International Speedway. Eleven months later his brother, Davey, suffered a fatal brain injury in a helicopter crash. Their father, Bobby, and brother, Donny, had previously retired from auto racing due to brain injuries that had occurred during races.

The velocity of external objects have the same influence on the extent of injury as the velocity of the person. Which object will cause a more serious head injury: a frying pan lightly tapped against a head, a frying pan dropped on a head, or a frying pan swung in anger? Again, the greater the speed at which the frying pan is traveling, the worse the injury. This explains why an angry bull, or even a baseball, can cause serious injury.

Five games into the 1984 baseball season, Dickie Thon, a promising young shortstop for the Houston Astros, was struck in the head by a fastball. Although Thon continued to play baseball following an extended layoff, he was never the same. When he retired in 1994, he was still experiencing vision problems and severe headaches.

The weight of a moving object also contributes to its force. Which will cause more damage: a pingpong ball fired from a cannon or a bowling ball dropped from a height of 2 feet (0.61 m)? In this case, the weight of the objects, not just their speed, determines the extent of injury.

A sharp object can cause injury more easily than a dull one because it concentrates the applied force in a small area. If you swing the flat side of a spade with all your might at an oak tree, you might

*All-star shortstop Dickie Thon drops to the ground
after being struck in the head by a fastball.*

barely dent the surface of the wood. Yet just a slight amount of force applied with your thumb can sink a tack into that same hard wood. That's because all of the force exerted against the wood is concentrated on a tiny, sharp point instead of being dispersed across a surface, as it is with a spade.

The hardness of surrounding objects also affects the chance of injury. If you fall off a chair onto a bed, you run little risk of sustaining a head injury. If you fall off that same chair onto a cement floor, the danger is greater. Being clubbed with a pillow does not produce the same effect as being clubbed by a baseball bat.

Therefore, any situation in which a person or objects around the person are moving quickly, heavy objects are in motion, sharp objects or surfaces are present, or hard objects or surfaces are present provides fertile ground for a traumatic brain injury.

WHERE THE RISKS ARE

Americans are most likely to be traveling at high speeds while driving or riding in an automobile. Not surprisingly, automobile accidents rate as the nation's number one cause of serious traumatic brain injuries.

More than two out of every three automobile accidents inflict some sort of damage to the head. Although motor-vehicle accidents produce only about one-third of all brain injuries in the United

States, they cause a majority of the serious ones—including nearly three-quarters of the comas. Brain injuries account for nearly 70 percent of all automobile accident fatalities.

Bicycles also increase the speed at which people travel. In addition, bicycling exposes people to the risk of high-speed automobiles without the benefit of protection provided by the frame of a car. More than 500,000 Americans receive treatment every year for injuries sustained in biking accidents. Brain injury, the most common type of serious biking injury, accounts for approximately 1,300 deaths annually.

Falls account for about one-fifth of traumatic brain injuries. The greater the height from which the fall takes place, the greater the velocity of the victim and the greater the chance of serious injury. Hardness or sharpness of surrounding objects also have a bearing on the severity of the injury.

At least 10 percent of all head injuries in the United States occur during sports and recreation. For some of these activities, the element of risk is part of their attraction. Each year, roughly 750,000 Americans seek treatment for sports injuries, and about one in ten of these suffers a brain injury. Approximately 5,000 of these brain injuries result in death.

The number of injuries in a given sport depends upon its current popularity and the built-in risks associated with the sport. For example, the number of brain injuries associated with rollerblad-

*These dazed Tour de France competitors prove that
even experts are not immune to bicycle accidents. In 1995,
one Tour de France competitor suffered a fatal head injury.*

ing has skyrocketed in recent years. Rollerbladers move at high speeds and are routinely exposed to hard concrete surfaces and heavy, fast-moving road vehicles.

Any sport involving high speeds carries with it the risk of brain injury from collision. Skiing, sledding, and motorcycle racing are prime examples, especially when hard objects such as trees lie in the path. Ice-skating can involve both speed and the hard surface of ice.

Other sports expose participants to the danger of falls. Hang-gliding, using a trampoline, and even playing on swings, slides, or monkey bars produce thousands of brain injuries each year. Due to the potential for falls at high speeds, horseback riding is especially dangerous.

Certain jobs, particularly in construction, can expose workers to sharp and hard objects, falls, and falling objects.

One cause of brain injuries that does not involve any of the apparent risks cited above is violence or assault. Violent actions account for 12 percent of the traumatic brain injuries reported each year.

The chance of a person sustaining a brain injury depends on lifestyle and location. Individuals who are extremely active and enjoy taking risks are more susceptible to injury than those who are less active and more cautious. Similarly, those who live in high-crime neighborhoods, have hazardous jobs, or live in heavy-traffic areas run a greater risk of

*An English jockey takes one on the head at the
1990 Grand National race.*

head injury than those who live in quiet, safe neighborhoods on lightly traveled streets or work at a desk job.

HEAD INJURIES BY AGE LEVEL

The dangers of traumatic brain injury vary with age. Infants have extremely limited mobility and cannot put themselves into high-speed situations as can other age groups. As a result, their brain injuries occur primarily through negligence or abuse. Sadly, child abuse probably accounts for more than half the traumatic brain injuries in infants. Infants' poorly developed skulls and muscle tone make them especially vulnerable to injury from shaking.

During the first 3 years of life, young children gradually become mobile and active. Yet they lack a high degree of balance and do not have the experience to recognize unsafe practices. Parents are likely to closely supervise young children in outdoor settings, while allowing them some freedom to roam in the house. As a result, indoor falls are the most common cause of traumatic brain injury in this group. Falls down stairs, from diaper-changing tables and other furniture, and while walking or running lead the list.

Older children are under far less outdoor supervision than younger children and are far more likely to take part in high-speed activities. As a result, the most common cause of brain injuries among this group is accidents during sports and recreation. Each year bicycling accidents send 400,000 American children to emergency rooms for treatment. Nearly 150,000 suffer brain injuries and 400 die from these injuries.

As with all age groups, a significant percentage of head injuries among children involve motor vehicles. But children are as likely to be injured while walking, running, or standing in the street as they are to be injured while an occupant of a vehicle.

Among adolescents, sports are the most frequent cause of brain injury. While injuries occur

Few recreational sledders wear helmets to protect against injury from hard spills and collisions.

more often in team sports such as football and hockey, head injuries suffered in individual sports such as horseback riding, skiing, and sledding are likely to be more severe.

Men between 15 and 24 years of age suffer more traumatic brain injuries than any other group. They participate in more physical and dangerous sports and tend to take more risks than females. Automobile accidents are the leading cause of brain injuries for this group, a trend that continues through middle age.

As American adults grow older, they tend to become more safety-conscious, less active, and less adventurous. The rate of head injury declines accordingly. But beginning at age 70, diminished physical abilities lead to more falls, boosting the rate of traumatic brain injury.

5

WHAT YOU
SHOULD DO

Jay was fortunate to have experienced such a sudden and severe burst of pain during the car ride home. It provided an obvious warning that something was seriously wrong. There was no doubt that he needed emergency treatment.

Victims of traumatic brain injuries are not always so lucky. Brain injuries are not like most other health emergencies. A broken arm, a burn, poisoning, a severe bee-sting reaction, or a deep gash all clearly require some emergency first aid, followed by a quick trip to the hospital. In most of these cases, the victims can provide fairly clear descriptions of what happened and what they are feeling.

This is not the case with most brain injuries. The skull protects the brain well enough that a person can often shake off the effects of the accident quickly. It also prevents us from seeing what is

Trained professionals carefully remove an injured person from a smashed automobile.

going on inside the head. There could be bleeding under the skull or swelling of tissue that is endangering the accident victim. Someone could suffer serious brain damage and even death if not treated within a few hours.

Unfortunately, a brain injury often renders victims unable to think or communicate clearly. They are often unable to provide much information about the accident or express how they are feeling. As a result, decisions about treatment usually have to be made without much input from them. This makes it especially important that people learn to recognize the more subtle warning signals of a serious head injury. Knowing what to do in case of head injury could save the mind or life of a loved one.

First aid is of little use for a person who suffers a traumatic brain injury. If the person is knocked down and does not get up immediately, the head and neck should be immobilized in case the neck and spine have also been injured. In all cases of head injury, the injured person should be kept warm and as calm as possible. Stress can raise the blood pressure within the brain, causing increased swelling and seizures.

Loss of consciousness, even briefly, is a clear indication that the person needs medical attention. The victims are often too dazed to know whether or not they have lost consciousness. Significant memory loss of events surrounding the accident is a strong clue that unconsciousness occurred.

Unconsciousness is not as reliable an indicator of serious injury in young people as it is in adults. Life-threatening brain swelling can occur in children and young adults who do not lose consciousness. In a recent case, a 17-year-old Denver high school student received a hard knock on the head during a football game. He never lost consciousness and so his injury was never noticed. The following week, his head collided with another player during a routine tackle. The impact normally would not have been severe enough to cause damage, but added to the undetected damage from the previous week, it produced swelling that killed the boy within hours.

Since consciousness is not always a reliable test, other factors should also be considered. Seizures, drowsiness, and vomiting are all signs that something in the brain is not working properly. The injured person should be awakened periodically during the night following a head injury, particularly if the accident occurred late in the day. If the person responds poorly to being roused or gives any other cause for concern, seek medical help.

Lack of alertness—inappropriate responses to questions, statements that do not make sense, inability to concentrate, general confusion, or slowness in reacting to situations—may also indicate a problem. Other possible indicators include persistent headaches, difficulty maintaining balance, loss of coordination, or any type of behavioral change.

The Colorado Medical Society advises coaches to remove from action any football player who receives a severe blow to the head and watch him for at least 20 minutes. If the player vomits, seems confused, or has memory loss, he should be transported to a medical facility.

Any person involved in a frightening or particularly violent accident that involves a blow to the head should be seen by a medical professional, even if the victim appears to display no symptoms. With brain injuries, it is always better to err on the side of safety.

6

EMERGENCY DIAGNOSIS AND TREATMENT

As late as the 1970s, most people who suffered moderate to severe traumatic head injuries died. Had Jay's sledding accident occurred at that time, he might have suffered the same fate. Certainly the consequences would have been much more severe because it would have been difficult for doctors to discover the deadly bleeding beneath the skull. Dramatic improvements in medical skills and technology have made it possible for medical professionals to assess injuries more easily and take steps to stabilize dangerous situations.

The first challenge facing emergency caregivers is to separate severe brain injuries from mild ones. They begin by measuring the patient's vital signs—temperature, pulse, and blood pressure—because they are regulated by the brain stem. Any irregularities suggest that the patient has a brain injury.

The medical staff then looks for signs that the nervous system, which the brain controls, is functioning properly. They check for dilated pupils and assess alertness, muscle coordination, speech, reflexes, and response to stimuli. They ask questions about the accident, the condition of the patient immediately following the accident, and whether the patient's condition is influenced by medication, alcohol, or drugs. If the patient is unable to provide coherent details, the doctor must rely on witnesses.

Nine out of ten traumatic brain injuries examined in emergency rooms show either no symptoms or very mild symptoms. The individuals are usually released without further treatment.

Patients who show mild symptoms create the biggest dilemma for physicians. Some experts say that all patients who show even slight symptoms of brain injury should undergo more intensive testing, just to be safe. Others believe that, in most cases, such tests do nothing but heap worry and a steep medical bill on patients.

Dr. Don Tandberg, professor of emergency medicine at the University of New Mexico School of Medicine, explains that, "With minor head injury, most of the [physical] damage occurs at the time of injury rather than from build-up of pressure on the brain."[2] There is no point in taking precautions to prevent damage after the damage has already occurred.

Doctors also note that a small amount of bleeding inside the skull will often heal by itself.

For these reasons, many physicians believe that it is a far better use of time and resources to keep low-risk patients under observation overnight or for 24 hours.

LOOKING INSIDE THE INJURED SKULL

Determining the extent and location of the damage is the next step in patients with moderate to severe symptoms. Until very recently, this was difficult. The skull provides solid protection for the brain, but it does so at the price of access. The same bony barrier that shields the brain from unwanted contact also blocks physicians from seeing what is going on inside the brain.

Prior to the twentieth century, the only way doctors could find out what was happening inside the skull was by opening it up—a dangerous procedure. Internal pressure could be detected only by outward signs such as bleeding. As a result, serious head injuries usually ended in death or severe brain damage.

In 1895, German scientist Wilhelm Roentgen discovered a type of radiation that passed easily through soft objects such as skin, and less easily through harder material such as bone. In the early twentieth century, medical technicians began using these *X rays* to take pictures of the bones inside their patients. Doctors continue to use X rays to detect damage to the skull.

Unfortunately, the presence of a skull fracture

Puzzled by the mysterious nature of the rays he
discovered, Wilhelm Roentgen named them "X rays"
after the mathematical symbol for the unknown.

does not provide much information about actual damage to the brain. The soft tissues of the brain show up poorly in X rays, as does the presence of blood.

An *angiogram* is used to check for injured blood vessels. If blood vessels leading to the brain are broken or clogged, brain cells may not receive enough oxygen. In conducting an angiogram, medical technicians inject a dye into an artery, and then use X rays to follow the progress of this dye as it travels to the brain.

EEGs, or electroencephalograms, can identify damaged areas of the brain by measuring the brain's electrical activity. To conduct an EEG, electrodes are attached to the patient's scalp. The brain is then stimulated and the electronic responses are recorded. Abnormal electrical readings to certain stimuli indicate damage to particular areas of the brain.

An important breakthrough in emergency treatment of head injuries came with the invention of CT, or computerized tomography. This procedure was first used in London in 1971. During a CT scan, the patient lies flat on a movable table that is inserted partway into the machine. The CT scanner then rotates around the patient's head, shooting a narrow beam of X rays at each of the dozens of stops it makes during its rotation.

Each burst of X rays produces a picture of a thin, cross-sectional slice of the brain. The images are then compiled by a computer into a three-dimensional model. In the process, the computer

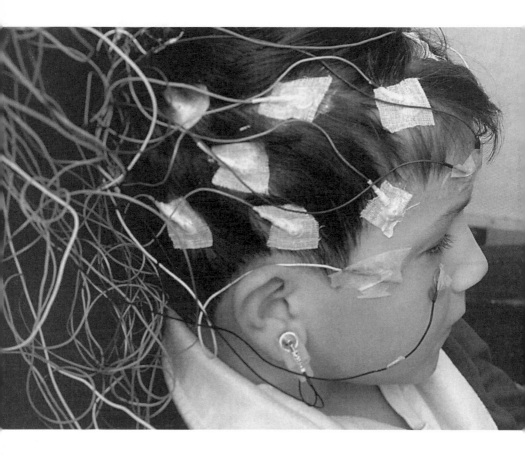

A patient is wired to EEG equipment that will record the brain's response to various stimuli.

eliminates the obscuring shadows that mar soft tissue images obtained using conventional X rays. The CT scan is a valuable tool for detecting hemorrhages and dead brain cells. Physicians routinely employ CT scans for any moderate to severe head injury to decide if surgery is necessary.

CT scans cannot always detect nerve damage,

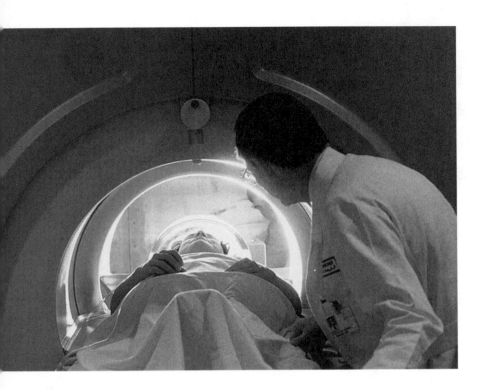

A technician slides a patient
into a CT scanner.

small bleeds, and tissue swelling. *Magnetic resonance imaging* (MRI), a more recently developed method, can show these subtle changes in the brain's soft tissue. It charts electromagnetic charges in a patient's brain by taking advantage of magnetic fields and radio signals.

By detecting bleeding within the skull, these techniques can prevent serious brain damage or death. Once the bleeding or swelling is located, a

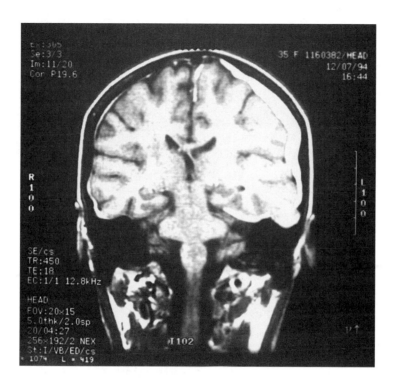

A magnetic resonance image (MRI) provides a clear, detailed view of a large area of bleeding beneath the skull.

neurosurgeon can cut away a flap of the skull to get at the ruptured blood vessels, seal off the bleeding, and remove the pooling blood that can cause a dangerous buildup of pressure.

Medical caregivers may prescribe anticonvulsant medications to reduce the likelihood of seizures. Sedatives can be administered to relax the patient, reduce stress, and promote rest. Analgesics are available to provide relief from intense or prolonged pain. Antibiotics are crucial in fighting infections that can easily occur in open head injuries such as gunshot wounds.

The most urgent task of any physician is to eliminate the danger of death and severe brain damage brought on by the immediate effects of the injury. Once that is accomplished, caregivers begin to think about the patient's long-range prospects.

The most reliable factors in predicting recovery are how long he or she remains in a coma and how long memory loss persists. A patient who is knocked unconscious for only a few minutes stands a far better chance of returning to normal than someone who has lain in a coma for 3 weeks. An accident victim who regains memory, coherence, and the ability to focus and respond very quickly stands a better chance of full recovery than a person who is still confused and wobbly weeks after the accident.

The area of the brain in which the damage occurred, the amount of nerve damage, and the general health of the patient all influence the degree of recovery. Young people often have greater recovery powers than adults, but this is not always true with brain injuries.

Taking these factors into account, physicians rate the head injury as mild, moderate, or severe. A case in which the patient loses consciousness for a few minutes and remains confused for less than an hour is considered mild. Loss of consciousness for several hours and continuing *amnesia* for several hours after regaining consciousness would rate as moderate. The case of a victim who has lain in a coma for more than a week and awoke with continuing amnesia for several days would be classified as severe.

These ratings are used to predict the long-term effects and may be somewhat misleading. Under these ratings, Jay's brain injury would probably be categorized as mild, even though it was as deadly as many serious brain injuries. The rating means that after the emergency treatment his outlook was encouraging.

More than nine out of ten patients who survive traumatic brain injuries are discharged from the hospital without further treatment. Half of them return to work or school within 3 weeks of the accident. They often resume their lives believing that the danger is past, and that they can continue with their lives as though nothing ever happened.

But an increasing number of people with brain injuries leave the hospital with problems that make daily living difficult. Ironically, medical advances, which have reduced the incidences of many health problems, have increased the number of people who suffer from long-term brain injury problems. In the past, many of these people would have died. Now they live, but many find day-to-day living a challenge. More than one-third of moderate to severely injured patients leave the hospital with one to three major impairments.

Many individuals who appear to have avoided major damage discover lingering effects from their injuries. One study showed that 25 percent of children with moderate brain injuries continued to experience decreased brain activity 6 months after the injury. Another survey found that one-third of the people who experienced mild brain injuries reported employment problems 3 months after their release from the hospital, while 80 to 90 percent of individuals with moderate to severe brain injuries were unemployed 7 years after their injuries occurred.

These problems often catch victims and families unprepared. Neurosurgeons who perform an emergency operation rarely have time for full explanations of what can result from even mild brain injury. The family is often just recovering from the shock of the injury and is overcome with relief over the escape from severe injury. As a result, patients are often surprised at the subtle changes that greatly affect the course of their lives.

7

LONG-TERM PROBLEMS

Brain injuries do not heal in the same way as broken legs or cut veins. If a broken bone is reset properly and kept immobile for a certain amount of time, predictable healing will occur. A bleeding wound on the skin will clot, form scar tissue, and heal, often leaving no sign of the wound.

Brain injuries, on the other hand, are unpredictable. Even with modern diagnostic equipment, doctors have difficulty assessing exactly which components of the brain have been injured and to what extent. There is no way to know how quickly or how completely a person can recover from a brain injury. Each case is unique.

Many of the long-term problems produced by traumatic brain injury are linked to the functions of the area of the brain that is injured. These are known as *localized effects*. To understand what can go wrong, it is first necessary to understand something about the geography of the brain.

The brain is made up of three main parts: the *cerebrum*, the *cerebellum*, and the *brain stem*. The cerebrum is the largest section of the brain. It is divided into two halves or *hemispheres*. The left hemisphere tends to direct activity on the right side of the body and the right hemisphere controls the left side of the body. Most of the activity performed

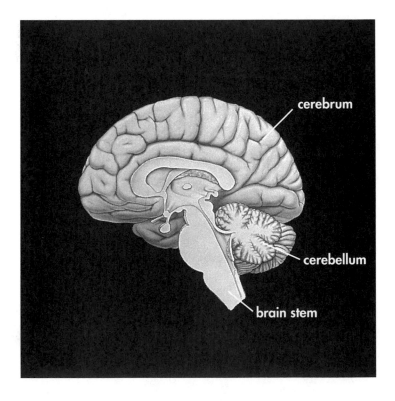

This illustration shows the location and appearance of the three main parts of the brain.

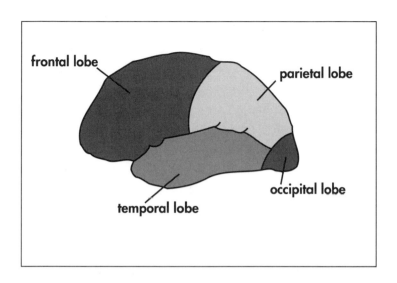

Left side of the cerebrum

by the cerebrum takes place on its surface, an area known as the cortex.

The cerebrum has four major regions, or lobes. The *frontal lobe* controls emotions, personality, voluntary muscle control, and the highest intellectual activities such as problem solving, creative thought, judgment, speech, and reasoning. The activity in the frontal lobe carries the primary responsibility for inhibiting impulses, providing motivation for action, and maintaining appropriate social behavior. Among other things, frontal-lobe damage can take a toll on a person's coordination.

The *parietal lobe* stores information gained from the senses of touch, taste, smell, and hearing. It also interprets language and is, therefore, used in reading and mathematics. Injury to the parietal lobes can lead to loss of taste, smell, or hearing.

The *temporal lobe* plays an active role in speech, musical ability, and memory. Damage to this area of the brain often affects speech.

The *occipital lobe* is the vision-interpreting center. Double vision can be a long-term consequence of damage to occipital brain cells.

The cerebellum is smaller and is located at the back of the head. It is responsible for remembering habitual muscular movements (such as shoe-tying and catching a ball), and helps in maintaining balance. Destruction of cells in the cerebellum can affect balance and disrupt a person's ability to perform basic motor skills.

The brain stem is located at the base of the brain. The stem connects the brain to the main power line of the nervous system—the spinal cord. It controls consciousness and arousal and coordinates vital unconscious activities of the body such as heartbeat, blood flow, breathing, swallowing, appetite, and thirst. Brain-stem damage can affect any of these vital functions.

Disruption of the electrical and chemical balances within the brain may produce seizures, especially in children.

ALTERING WHO YOU ARE

Some localized brain damage alters the basic mental and emotional makeup of the victim. This is especially likely to occur when the frontal lobe is damaged. This area of the brain directs many of the key functions that give a person identity: personality, inhibition, judgment, reasoning, and problem solving.

Other brain functions essential to our makeup, such as memory and emotions, may be diffused throughout the brain. Loss of these functions is not as easily identified with injury to a particular area of the brain.

A brain injury can rearrange many of the traits that define who you are. It can change how you act, how you react to situations, and your ability to think, joke, cry, and love. It may change so many of the basic parts of a person's individuality that family, friends, and even the individual no longer recognize the person they thought they knew. Even a mild alteration in the activity of the brain can influence how a person responds to life.

About 80 percent of people with brain injuries recover all of their physical functions within a year. Yet many of them continue to encounter cognitive, behavioral, and emotional problems.

COGNITIVE PROBLEMS

The term *cognitive* is used to describe brain processes associated with learning and knowing. The most common long-term cognitive problems affect memory. Although long-term amnesia is rare, people with brain injuries often have difficulty remembering recent experiences or new information because the brain loses some of its capacity to store or recall new information.

The problem is far more serious than the occasional frustrating or embarrassing memory lapses that we all experience. Because victims may be unable to remember what they have been told or have read just moments before, they may be unable to receive an education, complete job training, keep appointments, remember assignments, meet deadlines, or even keep up with daily routine tasks. At worst, short-term memory loss can trap people in a state of continual confusion. At best, it can erode self-confidence.

Disruptions of the nerve network in the brain frequently reduce the brain's efficiency. As a result, the ability to concentrate may also be affected. People with head injuries may tire easily, have trouble staying focused, and become frustrated. They may leave tasks unfinished, either because they cannot stay focused on the task, or because they lack the energy to keep going when the task becomes challenging. Coping with stress is especially difficult.

Brain injury can cause disruption of a variety of cognitive skills. Long-term problems of this nature may include learning disorders and problems with reading, computation, speaking, processing information, and understanding abstract concepts. People with head injuries may process information more slowly, and thus have difficulty following rapid changes of subject or dealing with events that occur suddenly.

One common intellectual challenge for people with brain injuries is performing *executive functions*—the ability to understand a situation, organize a plan of action to deal with it, and evaluate and adjust the plan as the need arises. Brain injuries frequently affect an individual's ability to think ahead and to understand the possible consequences of a planned action. Brain injuries may also limit a person's ability to learn from success and failure.

BEHAVIORAL PROBLEMS

The most devastating of the possible long-term effects of brain injury are behavioral changes. People known for a lively sense of humor may find they have lost their timing. On the other hand, previous personality characteristics may become more pronounced. For example, a person who was careful about keeping a clean house before an accident may become obsessed with the idea of cleanliness. Children and adolescents may take a little longer to shed immature habits.

While some behavioral changes can be attributed to increased anxiety and irritability over memory loss and lack of focus, more sweeping personality changes may be caused by frontal lobe damage. Behavioral changes are particularly aggravating because they tend to become more evident just as physical injuries are improving. In one study, families of people who had experienced brain injuries 5 years before reported that behavioral changes were the worst result of the accident. Another study involving more than 100 mothers of children with brain injuries reported that behavioral changes caused more stress than any other effect of the injury.

Some behavioral problems, such as impaired judgment, are closely related to cognitive problems. A person with a brain injury may use poor logic or interject statements that have nothing to do with the topic. He or she may become intrigued by ideas that make no sense. Understanding relationships between cause and effect may be difficult. He or she may be unable to show the appropriate degree of response to various situations. In one case, an Arizona man who had experienced a brain injury called police to report a missing cereal bowl!

In considering solutions to problems, a person with a brain injury may show a glaring lack of insight, overlook important considerations, and reach conclusions that the facts do not support. He or she may have particular difficulty looking ahead to future consequences of actions. This can lead to decisions that endanger safety or run headlong into financial and legal problems. As one *neuropsychologist* explains, "Because patients with brain injury can act impulsively, intrusively, or just plain bizarrely, some may get in trouble with the law when their behavior is misunderstood."[3]

Frontal lobe damage may also affect the development of social skills. A person's brain maintains smooth interaction with other people not so much by sending nerve messages that produce actions as it does by sending nerve messages that *inhibit* actions. The key to getting along well with others is the ability to suppress thoughts, actions, and emotions that society considers inappropriate.

For example, suppose you are in a hurry and a crowd of people is blocking your way. A natural response is frustration and anger, which may trigger the impulse to knock down everyone in your way. While this may be the most effective way of speeding up your progress, it is socially inappropriate. The frontal lobes suppress the impulse until you have had time to consider a more appropriate response to the problem. People who experience brain injuries may display impulsive behavior that puts them in dangerous situations and demonstrates a lack of consideration for the feelings of others.

Loss of inhibition is especially heartbreaking when it concerns emotions—another crucial part of a person's makeup that the brain controls. Injury to the emotion-controlling process of the brain can send people on an endless, wild roller-coaster ride of feelings and outbursts. They may laugh outrageously at things that no one else considers funny or cry over a trivial matter. Such people may lose their temper easily and swing wildly from one mood to another.

Personality changes can also be caused by damage to parts of the brain that influence the ability to be flexible. This leaves the victim unwilling to compromise with others or to adjust to new situations.

Thus, loss of inhibiting ability can reduce a mature, dependable person into a rigid, obnoxious, immature person with little ability to control his or her own emotions or actions. Family members and friends who would be willing to sacrifice a great deal to care for a person with virtually any other serious health problem find it impossible to tolerate personality changes. They may become angry at rude behavior and embarrassed by inappropriate actions. They may feel loss of affection for this inconsiderate "stranger" who bears so little resemblance to the person they knew and loved. Long-term studies have found that, due to their changed behavior, most people who experience severe traumatic brain injuries lose their former friends within a year.

Preschool children with brain injuries that affect personality are likely to be hyperactive, easily distracted, quick-tempered, and prone to do whatever pops into their heads without thinking. Or, if the brain sites governing motivation (also located in the frontal lobes) are affected, the child may be just the opposite: listless, unresponsive, and apathetic.

Older children may display many of the above traits in addition to nervousness, irritability, and social inappropriateness. Teens may display antisocial behavior that leads to trouble with authorities, especially if they made a practice of challenging authority before the injury occurred. Because teens are reluctant to admit problems and accept assistance from adults, they may be particularly difficult to help.

Adults with personality alterations caused by brain injury are often unable to maintain ties with friends and work associates. They may be less polished or courteous, or crude in their language and actions. Brain injuries can alter the very values on which victims base their behavior. Isolated from others, bewildered by their own actions, and shamed or disgusted by the type of person they have become, such individuals fall easy prey to depression.

INJURED SPIRIT

Everyone who suffers a serious illness or injury that results in long-term health problems undergoes a period of adjustment. The adjustment can be particularly frightening for people who experience the lingering effects of a brain injury. They must try to regain mastery over their altered lives with a control center that does not work properly. Sometimes the damage is severe enough that the brain cannot provide reliable control.

People who lose the use of both legs and arms have to face new challenges, but at least each is the same person as before. Nothing about them has changed except for the loss of a specific body part or specific function. People suffering severe brain damage must come to grips with a loss that strikes closer to the very essence of who they are. A part of their former identities may be gone, replaced by something else.

The comments of people who have had to cope with such a loss of identity demonstrates their bewilderment.

"I missed me!"

"I felt as though a stranger had taken over my body."

"I can remember looking into the mirror and not recognizing the reflection."

The loss of identity and loss of control over their lives can have tragic consequences. In an extreme example, a young Montana woman committed suicide after months of struggling with thought functions and behavior that had been disrupted by a serious brain injury caused by a traffic accident. "Over and over her lack of judgment and capacity for forethought led her into desperate predicaments," her parents wrote later. "Afterwards she could see what she had done and her self-hatred increased, but she could never seem to learn from her experience."[4]

To make matters even more difficult, people with brain injuries often struggle with their new situations in an environment filled with ignorance and even hostility. Because their injuries are often hidden from sight, other people expect them to act as if they were perfectly healthy. Instead of realizing that this behavior is accident-related, others may attribute it to immaturity and weakness of character. Authorities may not give them the help and understanding they need.

No wonder some medical experts refer to people with brain injuries as the "walking wounded." As one expert put it, "People who have been head-injured are hurting, suffering pain beyond human comprehension."[5]

8

REHABILITATION

The long-term outlook for people who survive serious brain injuries does not have to be bleak. Most people can learn to compensate for their weaknesses and adjust to new circumstances.

Early diagnosis increases their chances of recovery. Delays in dealing with the aftermath of traumatic brain injury can result in emotional stress and possibly even physical harm for the patient, the family, and those with whom the patient comes in contact.

Diagnosing the long-term effects of brain injury is not as simple as determining the immediate life-threatening effects of the injury. There is no laboratory test or procedure that can pinpoint where potential problems exist. According to Dr. Dale Thomas, of the University of Wisconsin-Stout Research and Training Center, "You can't say 'you've got injury here; this is what's going to happen.' Similar injuries can affect different people in different ways."[6] Brain-injury effects may be particularly difficult to gauge in children and adolescents because their behavior frequently changes, regardless of brain injury, as they mature.

Neuropsychologists try to assess the long-term damage from brain injury by looking for changes in brain function. They use a wide range of written and oral psychological tests to compare a patient's past abilities and characteristics to those of the present. Some tests assess cognitive abilities: intelligence, memory, use of logic and reasoning, perception, ability to understand consequences, ability to use language and a variety of academic skills, ability to absorb new information from both written and oral sources, and skill in organizing thoughts and planning ahead.

Other tests measure alertness, attention span, ability to concentrate, control over emotions, and psychological and social adjustment. And some tests look for specific signs that can relate an injury to a particular area of the brain lobes. For example, the ability to firmly grip an object is related to an area of the brain that controls muscular movement.

A typical neuropsychological assessment lasts several hours. The neuropsychologist compares the results with documentation of the individual's preinjury abilities. The doctor can then provide an index of the type and extent of changes that have occurred. The testing also provides an understanding of the intellectual, emotional, and psychological strengths that the individual can build upon in facing any challenges brought about by the injury.

REHABILITATION: PROFESSIONAL HELP

Once the condition of the brain and the effects of the injury have been determined, *rehabilitation* can begin. A program can be specifically tailored to meet the needs of each patient. It should help individuals recover as many functions as possible and teach them how to compensate for abilities that have been permanently lost. A physician should oversee the program, and be responsible for any medications that might be required. Although there are drugs that can reduce the likelihood of seizures caused by postinjury *epilepsy* as well as extreme cases of impulsive, aggressive behavior, these drugs may cause side effects such as reduced ability to learn.

Other professionals may be brought into the rehabilitation program, depending on the nature and severity of the injury. A person recovering from a very severe head injury may require:

- A nurse to supervise a daily health program that meets immediate health needs and helps the victims learn how to take care of themselves.
- An occupational therapist to help the patient relearn basic daily tasks, such as feeding and performing jobs around the house, that they need to function independently.

- A physical therapist to help the patient relearn or improve physical skills such as balance, strength, and coordination.

Physical and health difficulties, however, are not the primary concern of most people with brain injuries. According to Audrey Nelson, who specializes in working with people with brain injuries, the two most common long-term problems are finding and maintaining jobs and nurturing relationships with others.[7] As a result, brain-injury rehabilitation can greatly benefit from the assistance of the following:

- A psychologist can help the patient overcome problems with behavior, attitude, and relationships as well as the feelings of guilt, denial, anger, or shock that often accompany a serious accident. These feelings can hinder initial recovery. Psychologists can also offer relaxation techniques to help people with a brain injury deal with stress.
- A rehabilitative social worker is trained to recognize the challenges that a person with a brain injury may experience in society—at school, with employment, with the law, or with family—and to locate resources to help the individual deal with those challenges. The social worker can ensure a smooth transition from the hospital to the school for a young person with a brain injury, alerting teachers to the student's needs.

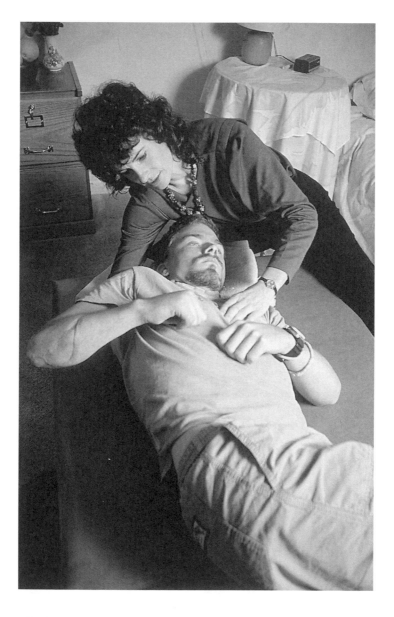

A physical therapist helps a patient with a brain injury regain strength and coordination.

People with brain injuries often have trouble with organization and can get disoriented or frustrated easily. A social worker can help a student set up a detailed schedule and system of checks as a reminder of what needs to be done. This will help keep the student from becoming overwhelmed.

- A tutor works one-on-one to help a student overcome learning difficulties caused by the injury.
- A vocational counselor helps steer individuals into employment suited to their abilities and needs. The short-term memory impairment that can result from brain injury makes jobs that require problem-solving, rapid transition from one task to another, or flexibility difficult. People with brain injuries often become frustrated and confused as they try to accomplish such jobs. They usually do better at jobs that demand specific, unchanging tasks such as data entry and word processing.

REHABILITATION: SUPPORT

The Texas Head Injury Foundation states, "A supportive family is the most vital asset a patient can have."

Immediately following an accident, family and friends will usually rush in with generous support. The family will surround the injured person with love and concern, and friends often go out of their way to provide the same assistance for the family.

Unfortunately, these sources of support may dry up once the patient is out of danger, because neither family nor friends understand what happens to a person with a brain injury. While people respond well to physical injuries, they often have great trouble recognizing and accepting the less-obvious effects of a brain injury. They are even less likely to have patience for personality changes or behavioral changes that they find irritating, obnoxious, or embarrassing.

Friends and family need to recognize that a brain injury can affect behavior. People with brain injuries do not act in a certain way out of spite or because they lack character. The friends and family of a person who exhibits behavior changes following a brain injury should focus on supporting the person's rehabilitation, instead of becoming angered by the behavioral symptoms of the injury.

Rather than confronting the person during a conflict, try to refocus his or her attention on something else. It is best to avoid arguments or speeches that are heavy on logic or reasoning—they may do nothing but call negative attention to the person's deficiencies in that area. Try to be confident, calm, and positive in your interactions. This not only reduces stress but also provides a constant role model of acceptable behavior.

Since people with brain injuries often have difficulty remembering what they hear, make a practice of writing things down. Use wall charts, memos, notes, and reminders.

People with brain injuries often have trouble staying focused and keeping organized. Their confusion and disorientation can result in a lack of initiative or purpose, and they may have trouble following through on tasks or assignments. Family members, especially parents of children with brain injuries, can help by providing supervision and structure. They can encourage the injured person to keep a schedule, for example.

Family members can also help establish a daily routine in which tasks and events are constantly repeated in unvarying order to help prevent confusion. They can check to see whether the individual is staying with the task and understands what needs to be done.

The family will generally take on the greatest supportive role. But the more people involved, the easier the rehabilitation. As artist Joan Carter observed, "If I could spread my needs among my friends, I wouldn't be too much of a burden on any one person, and I could feel as if I were controlling my life."[8]

Friends can also perform a great service simply by supporting the family. A brain injury can bring about adjustments in an entire family's lifestyle. In some cases, family members will become heavily involved in caregiving. The stress of coping with personality changes brought on by the accident may wear them out. They may not have much time

*Sarah Brady's support helps her husband cope
with his brain injury.*

or energy for socializing. Friends can be sympa-
thetic and avoid putting many demands upon the
friendship. They can serve as sounding boards for
family caregivers, who need to express their fears,
hopes, and frustrations.

Individuals with brain injuries and their families often benefit from joining support groups.

These groups reinforce the idea that people who experience brain injuries are not alone, and that they can build satisfying lives and relationships for themselves.

Friends or family members can educate themselves about the changes and challenges a brain injury can cause and offer reassurance that the victim is still of value. In an article published by the National Head Injury Foundation, a young woman with a brain injury said, "One friend who told me that 75 percent of me was better than 100 percent of others she knew will never know how much she helped me."[9]

REHABILITATION: SELF-HELP

Recovery is difficult to predict, largely because it depends so much on the attitude of the injured person. Some people may be unaware of the extent of their injuries, or have trouble admitting the changes that have occurred. They may fail to seek the help they need or even refuse it when it is offered. Others become overwhelmed by the changes in themselves, overly dependent on others, or mired in despair.

Anyone facing a challenge stands a greater chance of success with a positive attitude. Among people recovering from brain injuries, the greatest strides in rehabilitation are made by those who are determined to make the most of what they can do. They accept responsibility for themselves, but seek emotional support when needed. They deal with the anxiety by finding the information they need. A good source for both information and a network of support is the:

National Head Injury Foundation
1776 Massachusetts Ave. NW
Suite 100
Washington, DC 20036.

The National Head Injury Foundation has affiliates in virtually every state plus connections to several hundred support groups throughout the country. It can provide a wealth of information on all aspects of brain injury and it offers a toll-free number, 1-800-444-NHIF, to those who need assistance.

According to survivors of brain injuries, the most important thing that someone with a brain injury should do is to get information down on paper. This will help minimize the effects of the two most common problems of brain injury— memory loss and lack of organization. People who have experienced a brain injury can benefit by keeping lots of notes to remind them of details that might otherwise slip their minds. They should keep a written daily schedule to stay focused on day-to-day tasks, and a detailed calendar to alert them to coming events. To counteract the lack of motivation and follow-through, they should avoid words like "later" and "maybe." These words put off decisions and actions for another time.

Good health habits also aid in any type of

recovery from injury or illness. The body needs proper nutrition and rest to recover from injury, repair damage, and fight infection. People who have experienced brain injury should avoid using alcohol. When alcohol is absorbed by brain tissue, the brain loses its ability to efficiently perform functions including judgment, reaction, coordination, inhibition, and vision. These negative effects occur more rapidly in people who have suffered brain injury.

There is no set timetable for rehabilitation, nor a reliable method of predicting how fast or how much a patient will improve. The effects of brain injury usually improve most rapidly during the first 6 months following the injury. But a person may recover quickly from a brain injury even without rehabilitation, or may take a long time to show much improvement even under expert supervision. The person may reach a plateau, where little improvement occurs, or may continue improving for a long time.

People who suffer serious traumatic brain injuries rarely regain every level of functioning. But in virtually all cases, with proper treatment, they can improve with time.

9
ATTACKING THE PROBLEM

Brain injuries cause death in 70 percent of all fatal automobile accidents. Many of these injuries could be prevented or at least minimized by the use of seat belts. All 50 states now have legislation requiring that young children be restrained by a car seat. This law has greatly reduced the incidence of head injuries in children aged four and younger.

Many states also require older children and adults to use seat belts. Some people are reluctant to pass such laws or comply with them because they believe that such laws infringe on personal freedom, and that seat belts are uncomfortable and unnecessary. Others neglect to use seat belts for short trips or for traveling at relatively low speeds. Yet 80 percent of deaths and injuries from motor-vehicle accidents occur at speeds of less than 40 miles per hour, and 75 percent occur less than 25 miles from home.

Drinking while driving, another preventable situation, causes roughly half of the deaths from auto accidents and is the number-one cause of moderate to severe brain injuries. Recent campaigns to promote public awareness and strong legislation against drunk driving are beginning to improve the situation.

Motor-vehicle injuries that result from improper vehicle design and poor traffic or speed control are also preventable.

Motorcyclists, who travel at high speeds without the benefit of an automobile's shell of protection, are especially vulnerable to brain injuries. Many of these injuries could be prevented if the operators and passengers would wear helmets. Between 1967 and 1969, 37 states passed laws requiring motorcyclists to wear helmets. This decreased motorcycle deaths by 30 percent and brain injuries from motorcycle accidents by 75 percent. Unfortunately, most states have relaxed their helmet requirements in recent years.

Helmets could also prevent many injuries to bicyclists. Experts estimate that wearing a helmet reduces the risk of a brain injury by 85 percent. Unhelmeted riders are three times more likely to suffer a fatal brain injury than helmeted riders.

Helmets could prevent many sports-related injuries. They are required in many team sports such as football, baseball, and hockey. Although helmets are less common in individual sports, they could prevent many brain injuries if skiers, snowmobilers, sledders, skateboarders, rollerbladers, and horseback riders would wear them more often.

Houston Oilers' linebacker Robert Brazile shows why helmets are standard equipment for football players.

Another way to reduce injuries is to provide children with safe places to play. Children in poor, inner-city neighborhoods are far more likely to be involved in a pedestrian/motor-vehicle accident than suburban children. Playgrounds built farther from high-traffic areas could prevent some of these accidents. Many children also suffer serious brain injuries from falls, often from windows in apartment buildings. Inexpensive, lightweight bars have been found to cut deaths from such falls in half.

Increased protection, however, does no good if people do not exercise concern for safety. Nearly three out of four motor-vehicle accidents result from improper driving. Excess speed is a frequent contributor to serious brain injuries. Helmets do not eliminate the need for adequate supervision. Football players often suffer needless head injuries because they put too much faith in their equipment. They often use their heads as battering rams. Learning proper tackling techniques could prevent many of these injuries. Sledders need to be taught not to go downhill head first or to sled on dangerous hills.

The greatest barrier to preventing traumatic brain injuries is attitude. Auto-racing legend Bobby Unser, Sr., stated the problem that plagues efforts to reduce traumatic brain injury. "You always think it will be the other guy," Unser said. "It won't be you. If I were standing with just one other car racer, and we were told one of us would be killed in a race, I'd still race. I would be sure it would be the other guy."[10]

The "it can't happen to me" attitude explains why efforts to promote seat-belt and helmet use usually fall short of their goals. People do not expect to be involved in an accident. Despite educational campaigns promoting seat belts and helmets, millions of people refuse to buckle up or strap on a helmet.

Automakers have recently attacked the problem of seat-belt neglect by building air bags into the cars. Because this is an automatic safety system that does not require cooperation from the driver or passenger, it will do better than seat belts in preventing serious brain injuries. Even air bags, however, offer little protection against side impact.

Current technology has not created an equivalent safety system for bicycles. Bicycles pose an additional safety problem in that many older children oppose wearing a bike helmet. They say, "That helmet makes me look like a dork." Parents, who never wore helmets when they were young and don't wear them now, often give in to children.

This is why Andrew Dannenbery, a physician at Johns Hopkins Medical School, argues that education is "not effective unless it is combined with legislation."[11] Bike-helmet laws would eliminate both the futile parent-child battles and the social stigma that discourages children, especially adolescents, from wearing helmets. In Montgomery, Maryland, helmet use more than tripled after a law requiring helmets was passed. Helmet use among young bikers in parts of Australia jumped from 26

This family of bikers plays it smart by wearing helmets. Several helmetless bikers in the background are taking their chances.

to 71 percent after that country passed a nation-wide law requiring bike helmets.

Many of the methods for preventing brain injuries involve political solutions. The number of brain injuries caused by violent assault, for example, can best be reduced by attacking the problems of our society that spawn violence. Other techniques for preventing brain injuries often involve the creation of laws to regulate behavior. Seat-belt laws, air-bag laws, gun-control legislation, and organized recreational regulations all could reduce the frequency of traumatic brain injuries.

All of them, however, run into opposition on the ground that they infringe on a person's individual freedom. The subject of brain injuries is likely to continue to cause heated debate. Those who fear government regulation question how much power the government should be given to force people to act in certain ways. At the same time, others wonder why society should have to bear the staggering medical cost resulting from nonregulation.

AWARENESS

Human nature, the difficulty of changing society, and the degree of risk that comes simply with being alive guarantee that traumatic brain injuries will never be eliminated. Perhaps there will come a time when doctors are able to chart the workings of the mind so intricately that they can repair lost connections and restore damaged brain cells.

But until that time, the one thing that will most improve the lives of those who fall victim to traumatic brain injuries is public awareness.

Critical reaction to the film *Regarding Henry* illustrates society's lack of awareness about brain injuries. The plot of the film concerns an obnoxious, unprincipled lawyer who experiences a drastic change in personality (for the better) as the result of a gunshot wound to the head. Movie critics almost universally ridiculed the plot as ludicrous.

In reality, while improvements in personality are rare, the film's portrayal of a man struggling to adjust to a new personality so closely matched a real-life case that an Indiana man has sued the company that made the film for stealing his story.

Unlike most people experiencing health problems, those who suffer the lingering effects of brain injuries are more likely to get scorn than sympathy. Society spares little patience on people with behavioral problems who do not "look" brain-damaged. People constantly tell such individuals to "just grow up," or "just try harder," or "just pay attention."

The government often denies Social Security benefits to those who suffer long-term problems brought on by brain injury. Similarly, health insurance companies may refuse to cover the cost of rehabilitative treatment for people who do not have obvious physical disabilities. Even doctors may gloss over the long-term effects of brain injury. Some experts estimate that only 15 percent of the people who experience brain injury receive the treatment they need. Many medical professionals

Harrison Ford plays the starring role in Regarding Henry, *a movie about a lawyer who copes with a personality change after suffering a head injury.*

discharge their patients far too soon with overly optimistic assessments of the patients' conditions. Many patients return to school or work unprepared for what awaits them.

The schools are also unprepared. One study found that only 5 percent of special-education teachers, the teachers *most* likely to have some familiarity with the subject, received any information on traumatic brain injuries in their undergraduate programs.

Many schools do not even have documentation of which students have brain injuries. Less than a year following Jay's accident, not even his physical-education teacher had any record of his having sustained a brain injury. In Vermont, an informal survey of 1,500 special education students found that more than 20 percent of them had once been hospitalized with a traumatic brain injury. Forty percent of the emotionally disturbed students surveyed had a history of head injury. Yet *none* of their school records mentioned their brain injuries. If a student's brain injury is not taken into consideration, the student might be placed in programs that hurt rather than help.

Many people openly doubt claims that learning and behavioral problems are related to brain injuries. A county juvenile intake office in Wisconsin asks first-time juvenile offenders a list of more than 80 questions in an attempt to gain insight into the factors that might have led to the behavioral problem. *The list does not include a single question about a history of brain injury.* When it was suggested to a juvenile intake worker that this information might be helpful, he made it clear that he regarded mention of a brain injury in connection with antisocial behavior as "just an excuse."[12]

Many doctors ridicule claims of post-concussion problems as a way for a needy victim to get attention." In reality, neurological problems in such people are likely.

Lack of awareness can turn an already difficult situation into a tragedy. As an extreme example, consider a family who tried to get medical help for a 20-year-old woman who was suffering from emotional difficulties. The woman had suffered a serious brain injury in an automobile accident only 2 months before, and had been in a coma for a week. Yet the admitting psychologist refused to consider the accident as relevant. He dismissed her problems as those of "a little girl who didn't want to grow up."[13] Soon after, the woman committed suicide.

It does not have to be this way. People with brain injuries do face formidable challenges in arranging and focusing their lives, but in most cases, they can improve. As the public becomes more aware of the silent crippler, people who experience traumatic brain injuries will have better chances of improving.

GLOSSARY

acquired brain injury—brain injury caused by something other than an inherited condition or birth
defect

amnesia—loss of memory

angiogram—an X ray that traces the course of an
injected dye through the bloodstream. The test
is able to identify any interruptions in blood
flow.

anoxia—a condition in which the blood supply to
the brain is cut off, depriving the brain of the
oxygen necessary to keep it functioning

brain stem—part of the brain located at the base of
the brain. It connects the brain to the spinal
cord and controls consciousness and unconscious activities such as heartbeat and breathing.

cerebellum—part of the brain located at the back of
the head. It controls habitual muscular movement and balance.

cerebrospinal fluid—fluid that surrounds the brain and spinal cord, providing protection against jarring

cerebrum—largest part of the brain. It may be divided into four lobes or two hemispheres.

closed head injury—injury to the brain in which the skull is not penetrated

cognitive—relating to the process of obtaining knowledge

coma—loss of consciousness for a prolonged period

concussion—mild injury to the brain caused by impact of the brain against the skull

congenital nervous injury—abnormality of the nervous system that is present at birth

contusion—injury that causes bruising

cortex—area at the surface of the cerebrum, where most of the brain's activity takes place

coup contre coup—brain injury that occurs at the part of the skull opposite the point of impact because the brain bounces against the skull

CT scan—abbreviation for computerized tomography scan, a medical technique that uses a series of X rays to obtain cross-sectional pictures of the skull. A computer pieces the images together to create a three-dimensional image.

diffuse axonal injury—tearing or stretching of microscopic nerve connections and blood vessels

EEG—abbreviation for electroencephalogram, a test that uses electrodes attached to the skull to record electrical activity

electrochemical—chemical and electrical processes such as those involved in sending nerve signals *encephalitis*—inflammation of the brain due to infection

epilepsy—nervous disorder that results in recurring seizures and other malfunctions of the nervous system

executive function—the ability to comprehend a situation and prepare and carry out a plan to deal with the situation

frontal lobe—area of the cerebrum that controls emotions, personality, reasoning, judgment, creative thought, etc.

hematoma—a collection or pool of blood in an enclosed space

hemisphere— one-half of the cerebrum

hemorrhage—significant bleeding from blood vessels

learning—the process of storing information or thoughts for future use

localized effect—damage that occurs to a specific part of the brain as opposed to general overall damage to the brain

memory—the process of recalling information and thoughts

MRI—abbreviation for magnetic resonance imaging, a medical technique that produces images of body tissues by using magnetic fields to stimulate signals from atoms in the tissue

neuropsychologist—medical professional trained to determine long-term damage from head injury

occipital lobe—part of the cerebrum that controls vision

open head injury—head injury in which an object or

surface penetrates the skull and damages the brain

parietal lobe—part of the cerebrum that controls speech, reading, and math ability

rehabilitation—program designed to regain lost skills or functions

seizure—sudden malfunction of the nervous system

silent epidemic—term used by head injury survivors, their families, the National Head Injury Foundation, and other advocates to describe the lack of public awareness about brain injuries

skull fracture—a break in the skull

stroke—a condition that results from a temporary interruption of blood supply to the brain

temporal lobe—part of the brain that controls hearing, taste, smell, and speech

traumatic brain injury—brain injury caused by a sudden impact

X ray—radiation that passes through soft tissues but cannot penetrate harder objects such as bone. As a result, it can provide an image of a person's bones.

BIBLIOGRAPHY

Begali, Vivian, *Head Injury in Children and Adolescents*. Brandon, Vermont: Clinical Psychology Publishing Company, Inc., 1992.

Campbell, Kay and Constance Miller, *From the Ashes: A Head Injury Self-Advocacy Guide*. Kirkland, Washington: OPTIONS, 1987.

Closed Head Injury. Eau Claire, Wisconsin: Sacred Heart Hospital, 1991.

Corthell, David, ed., *Traumatic Brain Injury and Vocational Rehabilitation*. Menomonie, Wisconsin: University of Wisconsin-Stout, 1990.

"First Person Accounts," National Head Injury Foundation, (May, 1988).

Head Injury: Help, Hope, and Information. Albany, New York: New York State Head Injury Association, 1984.

Lash, Marilyn, *When Your Child Is Seriously Injured*. Boston: New England Medical Center, 1991.

Lehmkuhl, L. Don, ed. *Comprehensive Rehabilitation of the Head-Injured Person*. Dallas, Texas: Texas Head Injury Foundation, 1988.

Mate, Ken, "Joan Leal Carter: Art Heals Life," *TBI Challenge*. (Fall 1993).

Miller, Laurence. *Inner Natures: Brain, Self and Personality*. New York: Ballatine, 1991.

Rocchio, Carolyn, *TBI Challenge*. (Fall 1993).

Savage, Ronald C. and Gary F. Wolcott, eds., *An Educator's Manual: What Educators Need to Know About Students with Traumatic Brain Injury*. Southborough, Massachusetts: National Head Injury Foundation, 1988.

"Study Affirms Recreation Can Be Risky . . ." *TBI Challenge*. (Fall 1993).

Swiercinsky, Dennis P., Terri L. Price, Leif Eric Leaf, *Traumatic Head Injury*. Kansas City, Missouri: The Head Injury Association of Kansas and Greater Kansas City, 1993.

Terry, Christopher, "Head Injuries Scramble Lives," *Eau Claire Leader-Telegram*. (October 6, 1993).

Thomas, Dale F., Frederick E. Menz, and Daniel C. McAlees, *Community-Based Employment Following Traumatic Brain Injury*. Menomonie, Wisconsin: University of Wisconsin-Stout, 1993.

Warrington, Janette Moffat, *The Humpty Dumpty Syndrome*. Winona Lake, Indiana: Light and Life Press, 1981.

"Winter Head Injuries to Children Require Parents' Vigilance," *Rehab Update* (Winter 1993).

SOURCE NOTES

CHAPTER 1
1. "Athletes Push Aside Fear While Performing," Associated Press, March 1, 1995.

CHAPTER 6
2. M.R. Miller, "Medical Advisor," United Features Syndicate, November 3, 1993.

CHAPTER 7
3. Laurence Miller, *Inner Natures: Brain, Self & Personality* (New York: Ballatine, 1991).
4. "First Person Accounts," National Head Injury Foundation, May 1988, p. 3.
5. Donald Lehmkuhl, ed. *Comprehensive Rehabilitation of the Head-Injured Person* (Dallas, Texas: Head Injury Foundation, 1988).

CHAPTER 8

6. Personal conversation.

7. Personal conversation.

8. Ken Mate, "Joan Leal Carter: Art Heals Life," *TBI Challenge*, Fall 1993.

9. "First Person Accounts," p. 1.

CHAPTER 9

10. "Athletes Push Aside Fear While Performing." Associated Press, March 1, 1995.

11. Carolyn Rocchio, *TBI Challenge*, Fall 1993.

12. Personal conversation.

13. "First Person Accounts," p. 2.

INDEX

Italicized numbers indicate illustrations.

Acquired brain injury, 32–33
Adjustment, 75–77
Age as a factor, 46–48
Aikman, Troy, 23, *24*
Alertness, lack of, 52
Allison family, 38–39
Amnesia, 69
Angiogram, 58
Anoxia, 32–33, 35
Auto accidents, 41–42
    safety, 90–91, 93–94
    death, 41–42, 90, 91
Awareness, 96–100

Behavior, changes in, 22, 52, 71–75
Berry, Jan, 26
Bicycles, 42, *43*, 47
    helmets, 91, 94, 96
Bleeding, 35, 60–61
    cell death, 30

    detecting, 58–60
    small amount, 55
Boxers, 23
Brady, James, 26, 27, *86*
Brain, *30*, *67*
    geography of, 66–67
    how it works, 29–30
    protection, 31–32
    swelling, 35–36, 52
    vulnerable sites, 37
Brain stem, 37, *66*
    and vital signs, 54
Brazile, Robert, *92*

Carter, Joan, 85
Cell death, 30, 32–33, 58
Cerebellum, 37, *66*
Cerebrospinal fluid, 32
Cerebrum, 35, 37, *66*, *67*, 68
Cleaver, Eldridge, 26
Closed head injuries, 33–34, 36

Cognitive abilities, 79
Cognitive problems, 69–71
Coma, 34, 42, 62
Computerized tomography. *See* CT scan
Concussion, 34, 35
Congenital nervous injury, 32
Contusion, 35
Cortex, 35, 67
Cost of care, 22
Coup contre coup, 36, 37
Cruzan, Nancy, 26
CT scan, *16*, 58–59, *60*

Dannenbery, Andrew, 94
Death, statistics
    annually, 20
    cars, 41–42, 90, 91
    bicycles, 42, 47
    motorcyclists, 91
    sports, 42, 44
Diagnosis, 54–64
    long-term, 78–80
Diffuse axonal injury, 36–37
Drowsiness, 52
Dura (membrane), 32

EEGs, 58, *59*
Electrical impulses, 29
Electroencephalograms. *See* EEGs
Emotion, 69
Executive functions, 71

Family support, 83–87
Falls, 42, 44, 46, 48, 93
First aid, 51
Force, 38–41
Frontal lobe, 37, *67*
    damage to, 69, 72–73

Green, Ted, 23

Hardness and force, 41
Helmets, 91, 94, 96
Hematoma, 35
Hemispheres, 66
Hemorrhage, 35

Identity, loss of, 75–76
Infections, 34, 62
Inhibition, 73–74
Injuries, statistics
    annually, 20
    bicycles, 42, 47
    cars, 41–42, 47, 90
    falls, 42
    motorcycles, 91
    sports, 42, 44
    violence, 44

Jarring, 30, 33, 36
Jobs, as risk factor, 44
Judgment, impaired, 72

Kennedy, John F., 26, 28

Lacerations, 35
Learning, 29, 70
Localized effects, 65

Long-term
diagnosis, 78–80
problems, 65–77
Loss of consciousness
jarring, 30
length of, 34, 62
as symptom, 51, 52
Louganis, Greg, 23, *25*

Magnetic resonance imaging. *See* MRI
Medication, 61–62
Membranes, 32
Memory loss, 12, 23, 35, 51, 52
long-term, 70
short-term, 26
Mental makeup, 69
MRI, 60, *61*
Montana, Joe, 23
Motorcyclists, 91

National Head Injury Foundation, 88
Nervous system, 55

Occipital lobe, 37, *67*, 68
Open head injuries, 33, 34

Pain as warning, 49
Parietal lobe, *67*
Personality, changes in, 69, 72–75
Playgrounds, 93

Rating the injury, 62–63

Recovery, 62. *See also* Rehabilitation
Reducing injuries, 90–100
Rehabilitation, 78–80
assessment, 79–80
cost of, 22
professionals, 80–83
self-help, 87–89
support, 83–87
Risks, 38–48
Roentgen, Wilhelm, 56, 57
Rollerbladers, 42, 44

Scar tissue, 36
Schools, 98–99
Seizures, 35, 51, 69
preventing, 61
as symptom, 52
Self-help, 87–89
Sharpness, 39, 41
Skull, 56–64
fracture, *31*, 56, 58
Social skills, 73
Sports, 42–44
celebrities, 23
Stress and seizures, 51
Stroke, 33
Swelling, brain, 35–36, 52
detecting, 60
Symptoms, 51–52, 55

Tandberg, Don, 55
Temporal lobe, *67*, 68
Thomas, Dale, 78–79

111

Thon, Dickie, 39, *40*
Torres, Jose, 23
Traumatic brain injury
    case example, 9–19
    causes, 20, 33, 41
    kinds of, 33
Treatment, 60–64
Types of injuries, 32–37

Unconsciousness. *See* Loss
    of consciousness

Unser, Bobby, Sr., 93

Velocity, 38, 39, 42
Violence, 26, 28, 34, 44
    solution, 96
Vomiting, 52, 53

Warning signals, 51–52
Weight and force, 39

X rays, 56, 58